TEDDY WENT A-WALKING

A Rhyming Book for Children

about the Friendship of a Lovable
Bear and a Happy-Go-Lucky Dog

BY DAFNE NICOU ENGSTROM WITH JASPER

TEDDY WENT A-WALKING
A Rhyming Book for Children about the Friendship
of a Lovable Bear and a Happy-Go-Lucky Dog

Dafne Nicou Engstrom with Jasper

Published by: StardustBooks.net

ISBN: 978-0692591475

Design: Let's Write Books, Inc.

Illustration: Vladimir Milosavljevic

About the rhymes in this book

As you read through this book, you will see that the last word of each stanza has been colored differently than the rest of the words. This has been done to suggest that you purposefully hold back that word so the little one(s) you are reading to will be encouraged to come up with their own rhyming words or remember the highlighted word from a previous reading. This increases their participation, encourages their creativity and thinking, and is just plain fun. Enjoy!

4

Teddy and Jasper went a-walking,

Beautiful day, they were laughing and talking.

A bee flew by: "Follow it at all cost,"

Cried Teddy and ran, and in the forest got **lost.**

5

"If I find the bee's honey,
I could sell it for money.
But if I can't find Jasper, my friend,
This story will have a sad **end.**"

Frightened, Teddy met a dog.
He screamed, "You are a scary hog!
I'll run and hide behind that tree;
From you, awful hog, I'll then be **free."**

"I'm not a hog," the doggy said.

"I don't really know why you fled.

Come back right now from behind that tree,

And go for a ride with **me.**"

8

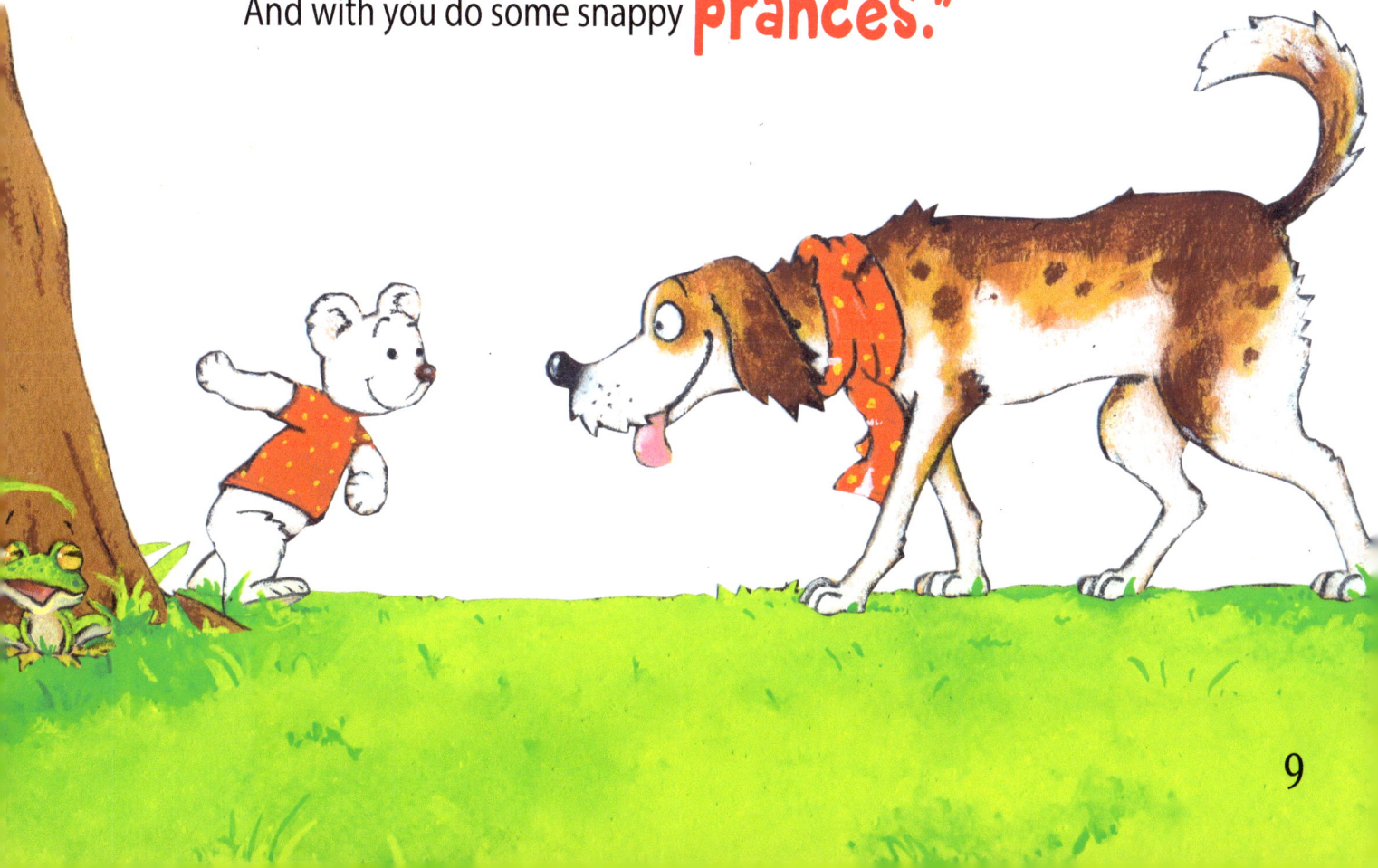

"How do I know I can trust you, dog?

I know no one here, not even a frog.

But I will take my chances

And with you do some snappy **prances.**"

The doggy said, "Swell," and, "Hello, hello.
I'm a nice dog, you know. Let's go, let's go."
Quick Teddy climbed the saddle up,
They then set out in fast **gallop.**

First they met a skinny sheep;
All her wool laid in a heap.
Cold and scared she ran away,
She hid behind a stack of **hay.**

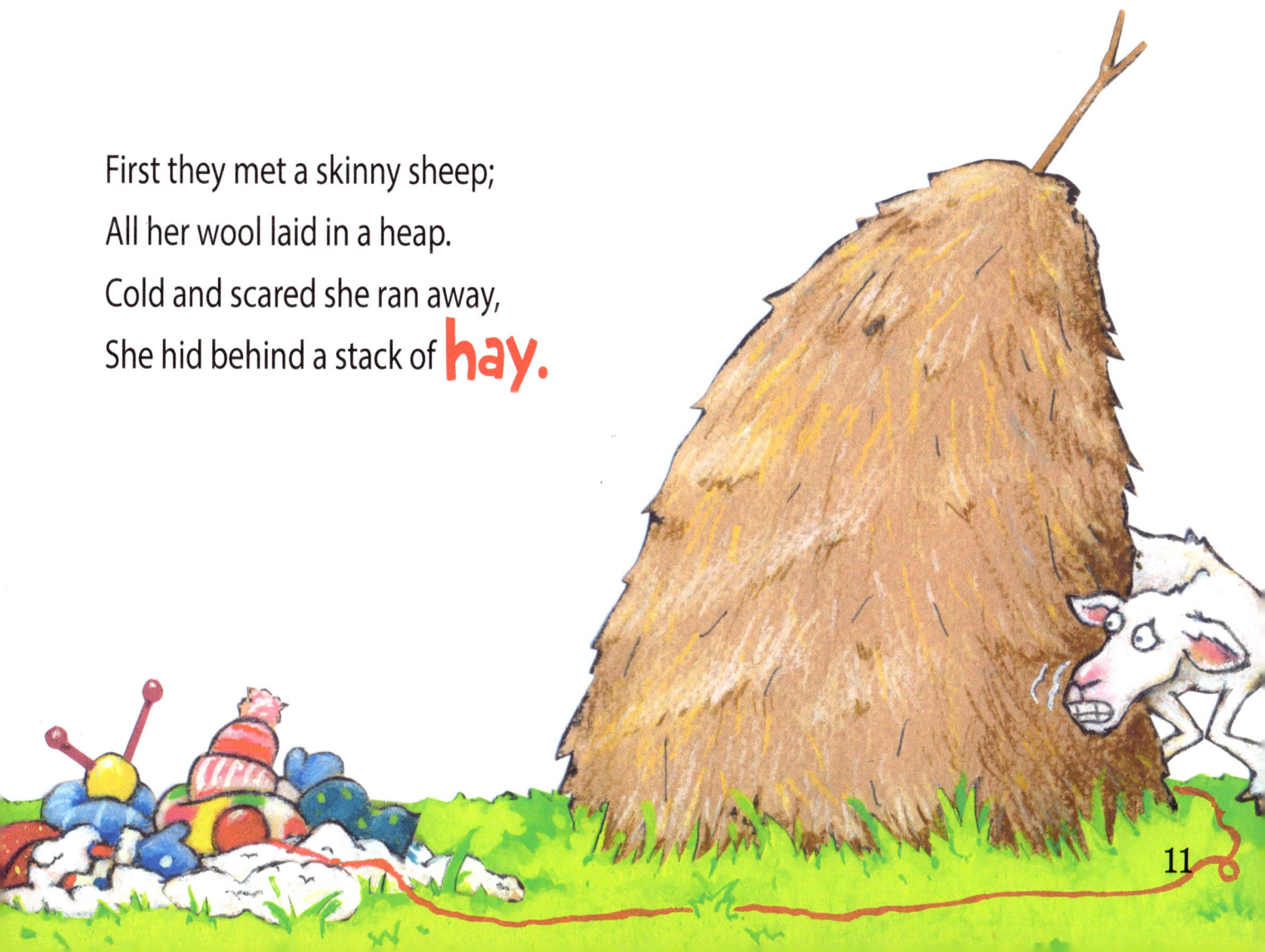

11

Then they met a big, fat hen.

She'd just left her egg-filled pen.

"Don't come close," her cackle said.

"My chicks are sleeping, deep in **bed.**"

Soon they came upon a lake.

Doggy said, "A piece of cake.

I can swim a solid mile;

Let's go out to that green **isle.**"

13

Many fish with fins that flap,
One jumped into Teddy's lap.
Swishing tail went *smack, smack, smack,*
Then fishy turned and slid right **back.**

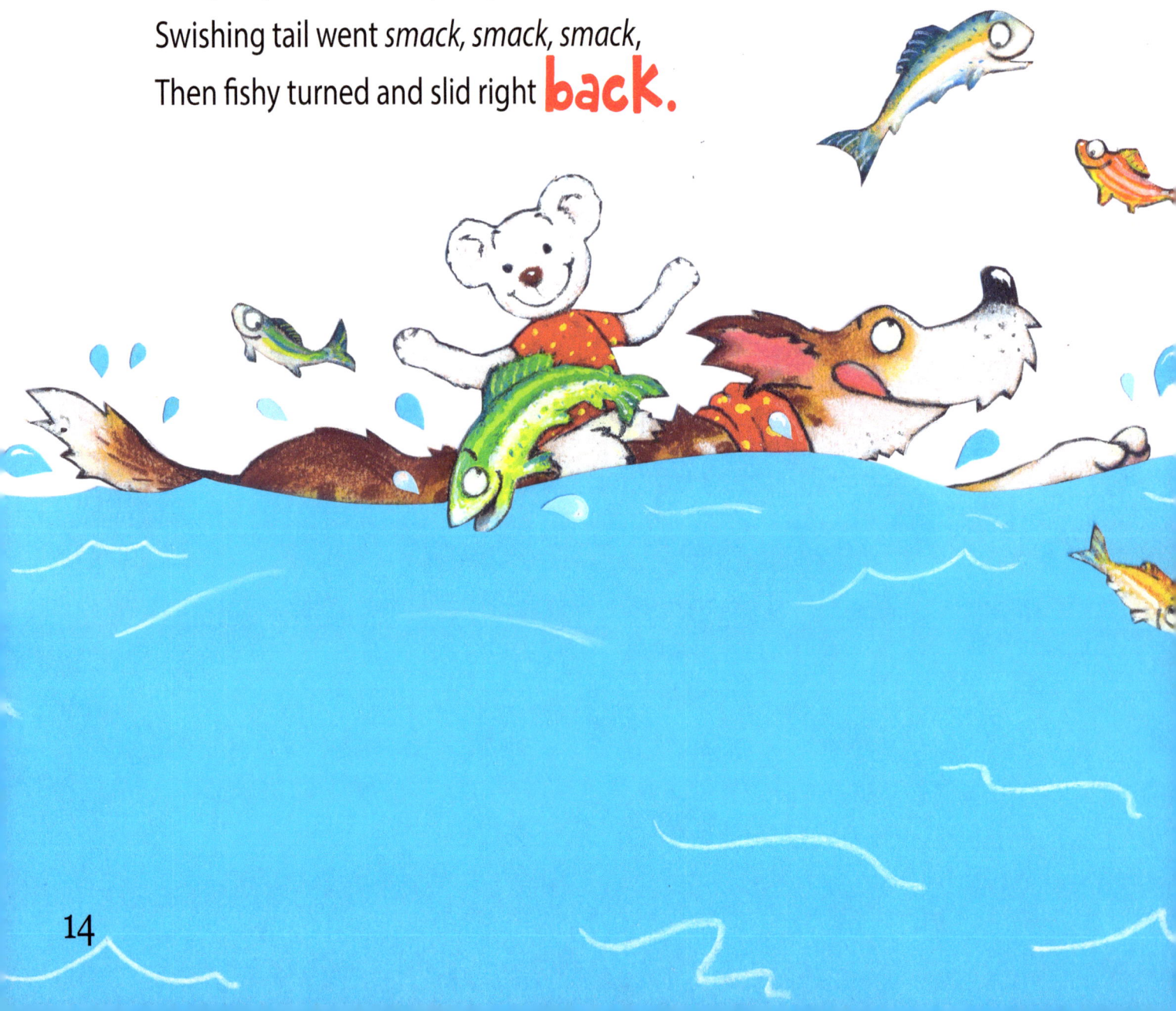

Now there came a crocodile,
Evil eyes and falsy smile.
He bit into Teddy's leg.
Teddy screamed, "Let go, I **beg!**"

The leg got bitten off in half.

"How awful," said a swimming calf.

She kicked the monster in his belly;

The croc, for pain, turned into **jelly.**

Out came Teddy's leg and paw
Doggy scared, but grateful saw,
That he could sew the leg back on;
It didn't have to be all **gone.**

Doggy used a thread of gold.

This, he knew, should always hold.

Mended, Teddy screamed, "Hurray!

Let's swim across the big, wide **bay."**

To Teddy's home they swam,

Happy together as one clam.

Teddy gave the dog a kiss:

"Don't leave me now, I shall you **miss.**"

"Come live with me in Jasper's home;

Without you I shall feel alone.

I have no place to call my own.

Said Alex the dog, "Can I bring my **bone?"**

Jasper stood waiting atop the stair.

"Am I glad to see you, Teddy Bear.

Bring your friend, come eat and rest;

We shall have a welcome **fest.**"

21

Dog and Teddy ate so well.
Dreamy eyes, they did feel swell.
They fell asleep in Jasper's chair,
A dog in love with a Teddy **bear.**

THE END

About the Author

Dafne Nicou Engstrom grew up in Europe during the early 1940's. At that time there was no television and certainly no Internet or IPad. What she did have was a large and loving family and they all cherished entertaining each other. Creativity was always encouraged and applauded!

During holidays presents were made and packages adorned, but most important was a card with a rhyme that came with each package to be read by the giver. Competition for the best poem was fierce.

There were also charming story books with rhymes where the last word of each rhyming stanza was held back and the kids in her family fought over who was first to fill in the missing word.

It is in this spirit that Dafne has created *Teddy Went A-walking*, encouraging the little ones to come up with the last rhyming word of each stanza: for fun and to develop their language and thinking skills.

Dafne is also the author of *The Adventures of Pee and Poo, The Fun Potty Training Book* and *Nico and the Ice Cream Caper*, a book about young homeless teens who succeed against all odds.

All of her books are created to be fun while offering inspirational life lessons.

Lean more about Dafne and her writing at: www.StardustBooks.net

Contact her at: Dafne@StardustBooks.net